The Hitting The Road Again Blues

Bob Hale

© 2011 Robert Hale All Rights Reserved
ISBN 978-1-4475-1090-1

Dedicated to

Elsie May Hale 1927 – 1999
and
Robert Hale 1924 – 2010

My parents.

Preface

All the poems in this volume are connected in some way with my travels. Some are about places that I have visited, things that I have seen, people that I have met. Others, while not actually about travelling were inspired by my travelling. Others were simply written while I was travelling.

It's a very mixed bag of themes and forms.

Over my life I have enjoyed every minute of my travels and I hope that in this small volume you will be able to share some of that enjoyment with me.

Bob Hale

Contents

The House On The Rock
    The House On The Rock
    Enclosed Infinity
    What Kind Of Person Would Live In A House Like This?
    Hemispheres
    The Golden Age Of Steam
    Looking After The Pennies
    The Devil's Carousel
    Streetwise
    Small Leviathan
    The Mikado And The Unseen Orchestra
    Inferno Part 1
    Voices In The Void
    Inferno Part 2
    The Doll's Carousel
    Dragons In Daylight
    Things I Never Saw

DPRK
    DPRK
    Outside And Inside The Mountain
    Flower Show
    The Glory Of The Leader

Sunsets And Sunrises
    Malawi Morning
    Northern Lights
    In The White Desert

Sunset On The African Plains
The Perfect Moment
Remembering Africa
Dragons

Small Dreams Of Travel
Iguassu
Machu Picchu
Bryce Canyon
Philippines
Guilin

A Brief Tour Of The World
Other Childhoods
Morning, 12th September, 2001
Morning At Lake Karukal
The Splendour of Troy
Feneos Afternoon
The Road That Runs Through
Waiting For The Holiday to Begin
Seeing The Sights
The Hitting The Road Again Blues
Bangkok Hustle
These Things Define The Day
On The Inca Trail
Haiku:Whale Watching In Alaska
The Invisible People of Prague
Alice In The Underpass

Part One: The House on the Rock

The House on the Rock is a museum in the Wyoming Valley. It was the brainchild of the rather eccentric Alex Jordan. It is an enormous collection of collections. Inside you will find everything from collections of paperweights to collections of church organs; from replica sets of the Crown Jewels; from whaling memorabilia to a recreated small town street. It can't really be described, it must be experienced.
This collection of poems was intended to give a flavour of the place. A collection of poems to describe a collection of collections.

The House on The Rock

Come up to the House on the Rock.
March by to the tick and the tock of the clock.
Come to marvel at mysteries, or simply to mock,
But come, nonetheless, to the House on the Rock.

Enclosed Infinity

There is no end to the line,
To the infinite, imprisoned, unchanging design
That stretches beyond and before and around,
Between Heaven and Hell, between sky and ground.
There is a world I can see,
But the glass holds it separate from me.
As I press my face hard to the cold
And watch this reality as the stories unfold,
The vertigo viewpoint succeeds
In feeding and watering the paranoid seeds,
And I think, far away, I hear music that plays
Metric and measured, a stately and slow polonaise.

Step into the House on the Rock,
Where time does not rule, there's no tick, there's no tock
Just the shifting and subtle illusions of shock
When you venture inside, at the House on the Rock.

<u>What kind of person would live in a house like this?</u>

Was it built? Did it grow? Did it just appear so
Overnight,
One night?
Did it spring from the Earth, did the Angels give birth
To this sight,
This delight?
There's a taste of the East, and a hint of the Beast
In the gloom
Of the room.
There are shelves filled with books in the crannies and nooks
But for whom,
Do they loom?
There are eggs made of stone, there are figures of bone
In array
On display.
There's the sound of a band but there's no mortal hand
Here to play,
For today.
There's a Tiffany lamp but it carries a stamp
There to show,
That it's faux.
It's a box of delights, It's a trick of the light
But the glow's
Getting low

What kind of person would live in a house like this?
Who'd dance with bogeymen down on the sharp precipice?
Who'd haul rocks to the top of the mountain and do it by hand
Just to see if the mountain would turn out the way that he'd planned?

Was it built? Did it grow? Did it just appear so
Overnight,
One night?
Did it spring from the Earth or did Nature give birth
To this sight,
This delight?
A man stands in the rocks. He's surrounded by flocks
Of strange birds
It's absurd.
All this bric-a-brac shines in a thousand designs
Till we're spurred
To find words
For the things that we've seen here and there and between
But there's more
To explore.
It's time to be going and we march on unknowing
To the door
The new door.

Come back to the House on the Rock,
To jewels and the gems and the schlock
To the weird and the wonderful stock.
Come back to the House on the Rock.

A collection of collections: Part 1: Hemispheres

In his house he had a case full of tiny Universes,

Of frozen explosions, of luminescent flowers,
Of slices of time and spirals of space,
All captured in hemispheres of glass.
He showed them as a child shows a mayfly,
Captured in cupped hands, precious and fragile,
Eternity trapped in a moment of grace,
Undying, unchanging, waiting for the world to pass.

A Collection of Collections: Part 2: The Golden Age of Steam

In his house he had a room where motion was caught
Behind a window in the wall, upon a shelf,
Where it became forever the Golden Age of Steam,
And the liveried engines stood in a trackless waste.
He showed them as a young man shows his car
Exuberant and boastful; this is mine, this is me,
See how I have taken hold of the dream.
See how I have tamed and conquered reckless haste.

A Collection of Collections: Part 3: Looking After The Pennies

In his house he had a wall where everything was safe,
Where the tokens of pecuniary hope were held
Inside minute houses and animals and heads,
Inside the tin-plate mechanisms of desire.
He showed them as an old man shows his treasures
Reluctantly, protecting them with the tightest irony.
These toys that should be holding are held instead;
Symbols of acquisition turned to objects to acquire.

Come along now through the House on the Rock,
Praise it in whispers, raise voices to knock
Stare at the strangeness that stands chock-a-block.
Come along now through the House on the Rock.

The Devil's Carousel

I will pass by the mouth of Hell
I will not ride this carousel
I will not heed the tolling bell
I will pass by the mouth of Hell

Above the circling angels see
The carnival that's tempting me
But I remain apart and free
While still the circling angels see.

The fabulous, fantastic wheel
Turns and turns to still reveal
Monsters strange, deformed, surreal
Revolving here upon this wheel.

I have no need of surpliced priest
For though I watch each prancing beast
That Hell's menagerie released
I do not need a surplus priest.

The fabulous, fantastic wheel
Turns and turns to still reveal
Monsters strange, deformed, surreal
Revolving here upon this wheel.

I will pass by the mouth of Hell
I will not ride this carousel
I will not heed the tolling bell
I will pass by the mouth of Hell

Streetwise

It's a small town in a bottle
In an everlasting twilight
Never quite escaping daytime,
Never stepping into night.
All the people have deserted
Their positions and their posts,
And the sidewalks and the storefronts
Have been left to twilight ghosts.
The horologist stepped out
Of his allotted time and place.
The clocks he left behind him
Fully wound and keeping pace.
The apothecary's gone
From his powders and his potions,
From his pills and panaceas,
From his liniments and lotions.
The barber's chair stands empty,
The porcelain is clean,
No blood stains mar the razor;
The shop remains pristine.
The fire truck's gleaming pumps
Are polished up like gold.
The firehouse dog is sleeping.
The fire-bell's never tolled.
In the sheriff's office
Stands the Head of Joaquim,
Pickled in a jar,
Looking shrivelled, old and grim.
The picket fence surrounds

The house at Main Street's end
And the visitor with half-closed eyes
Can silently pretend
That the past is trapped in amber
And this is somehow real
Not a fantasy of history
Built solely to conceal.

Small Leviathan

Carved on the tooth of a whale,

a whale,
a tiny perfect evocation
of the leviathan.
Minute whaling ships
surround it
and smaller still
deck-bound harpoonists,
have their arms back,
trapped in the moment
before the motion,
before the battle
with the beast
whose tooth
begins the tale anew.

The Mikado and the Unseen Orchestra: a poem for two voices
It begins;
the faint tinkling
of prayer bells.
Mannequin eyes
move in motionless
faces.
Gongs sound,
strings vibrate,
the wu-man and the pipa
join the mix.
A crescendo builds:
a rising cascade of sound
and fury.
The Mikado

It begins;
the slow drawn bow
on violin strings:
mechanical
movements by unseen
hands.
Cello
and viola,
timpani and piano
join the mix.
A crescendo builds:
An emergent symphony
of melody.
The unseen orchestra.

Come down deep in the House on the Rock,
Where the darkness holds sway, devils mocked
And it seems that your escape is now blocked.
Come down deep in the House on the Rock.

Inferno : Part 1

These monstrous engines drive the world;
The boilers, shafts, propellers, cogs;
The pistons, blocks, the pits of flame.
Around these loathsome shapes are curled
The paths where sinners creep like dogs –
Stripped of dignity, of pride, of name.
This inferno is the engine room,
The very base of base desire,
The foundry where all sin is made
And loosed to call all men to doom
And eternity within this fire.
Here are our weaknesses displayed.

Voices in the Void

And yet…
Even Hell must have light and shade.
Without virtue there can be no sin
And so the engines sometimes pause and fade
And still for a moment their clam'rous din.
So as the engines fall silent, one by one,
Then the void is filled with voices wailing
And when the tumult is, for an instant, gone
It might seem that even Hell is failing.

Inferno: Part 2

But then…
The hum begins again, the shafts resume their turning
And the sound of mighty organs accompanies the burning.
There is thunder in the darkness, an inferno in the hole.
There is everlasting pain in every corner of the soul.

Move up through the House on the Rock.
Follow the sound of the bleat of the flock.
Listen again for time's ticking clock.
Move up through the House on the Rock.

The Dolls' Carousel
"Oh Mother! Aren't they a dream?"
I hear a child whisper.
I do not agree.
This carousel of dolls makes me scream
At the frozen fleshless faces,
The eyes that do not see,
Following without moving,
Fixed on me.
I feel my flesh creep and die.

"Oh look at that tiny one! Divine!
Such gorgeous clothes,
So petite, so sweet."
It isn't sweet, I can't define
The way they make me feel,
Their rank and file, perfect, neat
An undead, plastic army
Of incomplete
Soulless homunculi.

Step out of the House on the Rock
And back to the world of the clock
Where time flows once, tick and tock.
Step out of the House on the Rock.

Dragons in Daylight
I have escaped into morning
But even now in daylight
I still see the dragons
That haunted my darkness.

Dream of the House on the Rock,
Of all that was seen, and all that was not
Of all you recalled and all you forgot
Dream evermore of the House on the Rock.

Coda: Things I Never Saw

I have walked inside a stranger's mind
And seen the flotsam left behind
As the tides of sanity receded from the shore.
I have felt the things a stranger felt,
Played the hand that he was dealt.
Was this a simple game of chance?
Was it nothing more?

I never saw the circus clowns.
I saw no sceptres, saw no crowns.
I never saw the planes and cars,
The butterflies and killing jars.
I heard no music boxes play.
They must await another day,
For if I could look for ever more.
There would be things I never saw.

The House On The Rock: Notes
Enclosed Infinity : Part of the house consists of a room that is built out above the valley. It's a strange cantilevered structure but strangest of all is that inside it gradually diminishes in size creating a false perspective and making it look as if it stretches to infinity.

What Kind of Person Would Live In A House Like This : The original part of the structure, before the complex of interlinked hangers was added, is the house. Inside the house there is a taste of things to come with an eclectic selection of items scattered around its unusual and fascinating rooms.

A Collection of Collections : The museum includes collections both large and small. Three of the smaller collections, represented in this set of three short poems are glass paperweights, model train sets and tin plate money boxes.

The Devil's Carousel : The most famous attraction on the whole site is billed as the world's largest indoor carousel. It's so much more than that though. The carousel horses have all been replaced with grotesque carvings of mythical monsters. Around the walls of the room are hundreds of carousel horses and above, suspended from the ceiling, are carvings of angels.

Streetwise : There is also a complete recreation of an old small town American street complete with a fire station, a sheriff's office and a row of shops.

Small Leviathan : One large hall is filled with whaling memorabilia, from the giant whale and whaling boat suspended from the roof to the tiniest and most intricate items of scrimshaw.

The Mikado and the Unseen Orchestra : Perhaps the most unusual collection of all is the collection of mechanical orchestras where invisible hands draw bows across violins and invisible fingers ripple across piano keyboards. Waltzes spring from nowhere, oriental timpani fills the air and everything merges into a surreal cacophony.

Inferno / Voices In The Void : There is a room lit in fiendish shades of red in which the collection of enormous church organs can be found. It is like a Dantean vision of hell.

The Doll's Carousel : The carousel of mythical beasts is not the only one to be found. There is a much smaller one on which dozens of dolls circle endless round. It's a very creepy and disturbing sight.

Dragon's In Daylight : When the museum is finished, the gift shop visited, the building exited, there are still a couple of interesting sculptures to be found outside.

Coda: Things I Never Saw
Much of the museum was closed when I visited so there were many things that I didn't see. One day I hope to return and see them all.

Part 2: DPRK

Visiting the Democratic People's Republic of North Korea is a strange experience. The trip was fully choreographed. We went nowhere, saw no one and did nothing that was not under the watchful eyes of our guides/minders. We were given a version of twentieth century history that is seriously at varience with that believed by the rest of the world.
It was a very disturbing place.

DPRK

I never saw a country as full of monuments
And as empty of hope.
I never saw a country as full of rhetoric
And as empty of scope.
I never saw a country as full of words
And as empty of truth.
I never saw a country as full of the young
And as empty of youth.
I never saw a country as full of the heretofore
And as empty of the hereafter.
I never saw a country as full of the absurd
And as empty of laughter.
I never saw a country as full of menace
And as empty of peace.
I never saw a country as full of the burden of life
And as empty of release.

One of the things we were taken to visit was the Friendship Exhibition, a labyrinthine complex built into a mountain and housing all the diplomatic gifts that have been given to the Great and Dear leaders. As a general rule the more elaborate the gift, the less respectable the regime it came from.

Outside and Inside the Mountain
Outside the mountain,
.....the ground was red and dry,
.....though a lowering sky
.....threatened rain.
Inside the mountain,
.....the marble halls were cold:
.....held their gifts of gold
.....in endless train.
Outside the mountain,
.....twisted figures – broken, bent –
.....through the gloom, went
.....about their toil
Inside the mountain,
.....silent soldiers watched with care
.....the treasures hoarded there
.....the monster's spoil.
Outside the mountain,
.....the mortal truth of brutish life,
.....of endless pain and strife
.....against all odds.
Inside the mountain,
.....immortal lies displayed in halls
.....by those who slyly call
.....themselves the gods.

We also saw a flower show. It must be one of the strangest flower shows in the world as all the flowers are either Kimjongilia or Kimilsungia and all the displays are themed around the Great Leader's birthplace or the country's various revolutionary monuments.

Flower Show
There are orchids of one type
And begonias of another
And they fill the halls with colours,
Though those colours number - two!
You may search from end to end
If you're looking for some other,
But this purple and this red
Are the only ones on view.
It's a flower show with a difference;
It's a duo of varieties;
One named for each leader
The Dear One and the Great.
A tulip or a daffodil
Would be an impropriety,
Such a thing in such a flower show
Would be to desecrate.
Kimilsungia, Kimjongilia
Which are counted by the ton
Surround models of the birthplace
Of the leader - Mangyindae
Or occasionally a statue -
A revolutionary one -
Being all that all the entrants
Are permitted to display.

Then there was the children's show. This was an all-singing, all dancing extravaganza celebrating the Great Leader's birthday. It was bright, colourful, exceptionally well done and utterly chilling.

The Glory of the Leader

Bells all rang, for the glory of the leader.
Children sang, for the glory of the leader,
And they danced, for the glory of the leader,
All entranced, by the glory of the leader.
The band played on, for the glory of the leader.
The choir swayed along, for the glory of the leader.
Flowers were grown, for the glory of the leader,
And plucked and shown, for the glory of the leader.

Statues were carved, for the glory of the leader,
While people starved, for the glory of the leader.
And they feared, the glory of the leader.
Some disappeared, for the glory of the leader.
Missiles flew, for the glory of the leader.
Tensions grew, for the glory of the leader.
Hope one day, that the glory of the leader,
Doesn't make us pay, for the glory of the leader.

Part 3: Sunsets and Sunrises

I love sunsets and sunrises. I love to watch them. I love to photograph them. I love to describe them in prose and I love to write poems about them.

Malawi Morning

Walking through the morning,
driven to unaccustomed insomniac meandering
by the orchestra of snoring in the dormitory,
I watched an unfamiliar sun rise above an unfamiliar horizon.
It lifted itself through a perfect arc,
Unglued itself from the jagged mountain line.
Dragged itself inch by careful inch until it was free of the ground,
Balanced on a cushion of blue sky.

Walking through the morning,
awake and alone, the only human figure in the landscape,
as daybreak bled colour into the monochrome traces of night.
I listened to unfamiliar birds sing their unfamiliar morning hymns.
Some sang with booming, echoing, joyous whoops.
Some sang with cascading, waterfalls of notes.
Some sang with screeches, squawks or witches cackles:
And then, suddenly, there was silence.

Walking through the morning,
I waited, as Africa awoke.
One night in Iceland we were treated to the most magnificent display of the Northern Lights. The next morning I rose early and walked around the eerie landscape as the sun rose.

Northern Lights
There are no lights in the sky now
save for the bullying sun
threatening the faintest of faint clouds
that cling to the horizon
unwilling to let go
fearing oblivion.
Ghosts of steam escape the underworld
to haunt the rocks and hollows
to drift across the empty land
lost, lonely, spectral things,
pale dancers pirouetting
in the daylight.
Since last night the world has changed
for then there were flames and fire
ghosts above us rather than around
angels in a hollow sky
reaching into our hearts
from eternity.
Silk circles wrapped around the world
rippled and shifted and shook
and shrank to faint lace traces
that glowed more brightly as they died
leaving the sky a deep
and empty black.

Perhaps the greatest way to wake up is out of doors, in the desert, watching the sun climb slowly over the horizon.

In The White Desert

Awake on the bone ground
In shattered geometries of stone
Alone, surrendered to the night,
In the White Desert
Starfish stranded, darkness bound
The centre of the silent dome
Of scattered, ancient frozen lights
In the White Desert

A falling star, a spark
Ignites the breaking fire
Pours flame over the circling heights
Into the White Desert
Drives wedges through the dark
Until it's clutching hand expires
And reveals again the sight
Of the White Desert.

And if that's the best kind of sunrise then surely the best kind of sunset must be to sit out on the African plains, sipping a cold beer, watching a distant line of elephants march slowly past as the sun slowly dips below the horizon.

Sunset on the African Plains

The alchemy of sunset turns leaden clouds to gold,
Sets shadow fires among the trees as twilight takes a hold.
The plains are never silent, but now every hoot and howl,
Every shriek and roar and below, every cackle, every growl
Echoes through the world, like the cries of wandering souls,
And towards, around and through us, onward the thunder rolls.
But then the sun has gone, the clouds are black in black
And a kind of quiet falls along each darkened track.
It's a quiet filled with whispers and the rustling of grass
As beasts that hid in daylight disturb us as they pass.
And now and then a distant roar cuts off distant cries
As one creature finds a meal and another creature dies.
There is beauty in the symmetry, but a beauty fierce and raw,
That the march of day and night can only underscore.

I once sat for over an hour on a hotel balcony in Laos looking out across the Mekong River. I was fascinated by the ever changing colours and textures of the scene and, at just the perfect moment I took a photograph.

The Perfect Moment

Waiting for the perfect moment,
for the sun to touch the ground.
Waiting as the birds' strange songs
counterpoint the river's soothing sound.
Waiting in a broken wicker chair.
Waiting on the balcony, sipping tea.
Waiting for the perfect moment,
there is my camera and there's me.

Colour creeps into the faded sky,
and out of the fading land.
The trees that frame the golden water
become blackened where they stand,
and the sun is, for a moment, balanced
where mountains from horizon climb
and the perfect moment comes, and goes;
a single shutter-click of time.

Two Nights: Two Days - Remembering Africa

Here, now,
the sky is empty
and not even black,
merely a darker grey.
The stars are gone
lost in the eternal twilight
of the technological world.
There, then,
the sky was crowded,
a million sequins
on a velvet cloth.
The stars eternal
were spirits of the night
and the land was empty.
Here, now,
the city screams
and the heat smells
of machinery.
The sun is gone
lost behind the haze
in a hidden sky.
There, then,
the plains murmured
and the heat smelled
of animals and dirt.
The sun was god
ruling a sharper world
from a lonely sky.

One morning, in Turkey, I rose early for a walk along the beach. In the sky there were two hang gliders.

Dragons

Above the sea two dragons fight
Their wings ablaze with morning light
They swoop they dive, they turn and soar
Two titans in balletic war.

Red, about to win the day
Without warning falls away
And Blue, quick with Angelic grace
Dips sharply down to give the chase.

Skimming on the waves they come
Towards the shore they're driven on.
Together as they reach the sand
In silent symmetry they land.

And the men who took them to the sky
Shed their wings - the dragons die.
Become only silk upon a frame
Their dragon fight a human game.

Part 5: Small dreams of travel

1. Iguassu

Below I hear the thunder roar,
While in the sky I turn and soar,
Become the spirit of the air
Escape the Gods of Water's Lair.

2. Machu Picchu

The morning mists that hide the view
Have filled the world with silence too,
But here and there the cover breaks
And ancient Machu Picchu takes
The centre stage in my mind's eye.
I, from the Sun Gate, watch and sigh.

3. Bryce Canyon

The world is full of twisted spires
In hues of roses, berries, fires.
The path I tread that weaves between
The maze-like walls, the deep ravine,
Is lit by random fractured light -
Here dark, there light, here dark, there light.
The canyon's rocks like dancers stand
In frozen stately saraband.

4. Philippines
A fire is set upon the sand
And in the dark she holds my hand.
I want to turn to see her face,
But time has fixed me in my place.

5. Guilin
The boat is long and low and wide,
The water grey and slow: we glide
Through mountains mirrored low and high
Upon the river that holds the sky.

Notes:

1. I walked on the wooden paths that they have built in the safer parts of the falls, I approached the thundering cataract in a boat, I descended through the trees on the tracks to approach the base where the noise made all thought of speech impossible and the spray soaked me to the skin in the space of a single heartbeat - but best of all I flew high above the falls in a helicopter and saw them in all their glory, as if a Titan's axe had been smashed into the ground and then lifted to leave a raw and gaping wound in the planets side.

2. We reached the Sun Gate before dawn, hiking up the last few kilometres of the Inca trail in the dark. We stood, breathless and eager, and waited for the dawn. Mist covered the ruins, stole the view and deadened all sound. Here and there, now and again, it parted, gave a tantalising view of the ruins and I imagined them as they

might have been, covered in gold, full of the buzz of a living city waking to a new day.

3. A row of rocks that looked like musicians turned to stone lined the rim of Bryce Canyon. Turning around I saw another that looked for all the world like a pedestal with a civic statue of Queen Victoria. Everything was in shades of red, everything looked like roses or berries or fire. The path was smooth and flat and even and took me through an alien landscape, through a Martian wonderland. Or perhaps, as the morning sun turned the twisted rock to flames, the road to hell.

4. In the distance there was a fire on the sand and people trying to celebrate the new year with fireworks. We sat at the end of the beach on a log and held hands in silence. There was the soft lapping sound of the waves, the faint rustle of the trees behind us. And now, even in the dreams, I am almost unable to recall her face. Perhaps I will have the dream again and be able to turn to see her. Or perhaps not.

5. The Karst scenery rose all around us like the molehills of the gods. The water was slow as the boat drifted along the surface. I played counting games with a Chinese girl who knew only the numbers in English. The water was a perfect reflection of the mountains and the sky. Cormorant fisherman watched from the shallows, villagers watched from the shore. We watched them watching us.

Part 6: A brief tour of the world

The poems in this section are from my travels in many different places and are on many different themes.

The first was from a visit to a temple in rural Pakistan.

Other Childhoods

Black oil, thicker than blood;
thicker than treacle; thick as paste;
forcing its way through the crack in the pipe;
gathering in globules, in shiny tumescences
around the ragged edge of the metal.
Viscosity battling gravity,
overcoming it for a time,
but finally – with a sucking, slurping sigh –
quitting the struggle; dropping into the spreading pool;
spreading into the dust;
toxic ink on a sandy blotter.

And there, dirt-clad and dust-grey,
a naked child drew patterns in the foulness
with tiny questing fingers.
Oblivious to the stench, oblivious to the danger,
oblivious to the poison, he wiped it into his skin,
into his hands, his arms, his face.

And no one stopped him;
not his mother, sitting yards away
on the mud step of a mud house,
washing vegetables in ditch-dirty water;
not his brothers and sisters and playmates
absorbed in their own games,
their own worlds of childhood;
not the barefoot beggars, the silent supplicants
who passed him by unseeing and unheeding;
and not us, viewing from the cracked window
of the bus as we followed them down to the temple
and left him there.

Perhaps the grimmest inspiration for a poem came when I was in Laos and rose one morning to hear the news about the attack on the World Trade Centre. We were visiting a small village that day but it all took on a rather different aspect in the wake of that event. As some of the group went for a boar trip, I sat in the corner of the village watching and writing.

Morning, 12th September 2001

Thin rain turned the dusty ground a slick yellow,
Darkened the wood of the huts where the villagers stood
Watching with curious eyes moving in unmoving faces.
A hen fluttered from beneath the temple's stone steps.
Two monks in orange robes unshuttered the windows.
A pig grunted, a donkey brayed,
A duckling took shelter beneath our truck.
There was comfort in the mundanity,
Of a world shrunk to just this moment.

I saw three turkeys kill a chick,
Rip it, tear at its fragile featherless body,
Toss it into the air, dash it against the ground,
Then leave it, twitching, bleeding, dying.
The rain washed and watered it,
Diluted the trickle of thin pale blood,
Washed away the traces of its brief life.
I watched with no understanding
Of this alien avian cruelty.
I could not bear to see its pain.
I took a stone and broke its neck.

Sometimes only words can really capture the essence of a moment.

Morning at Lake Karukal
I need a mystic camera
to capture the moment, hold it forever
in an amber slice of time.
I need to capture the infinite
shades of brown and green
of the grass, the moss, the pine.
I need to capture the sun
that paints diamonds on the river
and stripes upon the ground.
I need to capture the gathered gloom
as I look towards the hill
where the trees are huddled round.
I need to capture the chattering
whining, buzzing of the insects
hanging unseen in the air;
the ever changing never changing
murmur of the tumbling water
that cascades down natures stair.
I need to capture the morning smell
of hay, and summer and rotting wood
and the warming earth
and the still calm tranquillity
of this moment in the mountains
this new day's birth.

I have my mystic camera -
the words that stir the memory,
the words that try
to re-conjure with a phrase the moment.
I have the perfect mystic camera,
the lens of the mind's eye.

I've visited many different historical and archaeological sites. One of them, Troy, is located in what is now Turkey but it is a very ancient city – or rather a series of very ancient cities.

<u>The Splendour of Troy</u>
Nine cities stood here -
three thousand years
of life and war -
the belief of every man
that they would stand
three thousand more.
Now there are only hills
and those who still
will seek to cast,
among mud and stone,
and blood and bone,
an image of the past.
But I see mounds of Earth,
no signs of ancient worth
just sad decay
and the truest story
that every glory
must pass away.

Hiking in Greece, I twisted my knee and was forced to rest for a day in Feneos.

Feneos Afternoon
Imprisoned in the village
I waited for my friends.
Trapped in my monoglot silence
I was a stranger to these people,
trying so hard to be kind
to the injured hiker.
Grandmother mimed a chicken
and gave me eggs for lunch.
Grandfather silently handed me
bottles of beer.
I tried to read my borrowed book,
but the heat stole my will,
made me one with the quiet
still old men of the place.
One of them handed me
a cube of Turkish Delight,
wrapped in paper.
Its sweetness coiled
And writhed in my mouth.
As the sunlight drained from the sky
my friends arrived
and I turned English again,
and the villagers withdrew
from our noise and foreign humours.
Tomorrow, healed and rested,
I would move on from here,
but for one day I had been
another figure in a landscape.

This set of four poems was written for a competition for poems to display on the Metro. The Hitting The Road Again Blues was one of the runners up and was displayed for a couple of months.

Four Short Poems About Travel

The road that runs through
Under my skin the itching is growing
I've spent too long here, it's time to be going.
I have to be moving, and I really don't care
Where the road leads or how I'll get there.
It isn't important, my next port of call.
The motion's the thing, the journey is all.
Though the mountains and deserts are wondrous to see
It's the road that runs through them that's important to me.

Waiting For the Holiday To Begin
There's a family on the platform,
A man, a woman, two children
Lots of suitcases.
The little girl is throwing stones
At her brother
Who is pulling faces.
The man looks at his watch,
Then up and down the track,
But there's no train.
The boy, with concentration asks
"If this is a holiday.
Where's the rain ?"

Seeing the Sights

Been there, done that, can't you see the T-shirt ?
Round the World, and back,
Carrying a rucksack.
Sometimes, a hotel, a night of comfort doesn't hurt.
Here and there, everywhere,
Off and on the beaten track.
Deserts, jungles, from the mountains to the sea
Waterfalls, glaciers
I passed them on my way
Great Wall, Pyramids, every sight there is to see
The White House, Taj Mahal
I've seen them for a day.

The Hitting The Road Again Blues

I got the dirt track, dust bowl, hit the road again blues.
It's time to put back on my boots, lose my city shoes.
The road is singing its siren song for me
It's only when I'm movin' that I'm ever really free.
I got the dirt track, dust bowl, hit the road again blues.
If I stay here in the city, I think I'm gonna blow a fuse
I have places to go, I have things I gotta see
It's only when I'm moving that I know who I want to be..
I got the dirt track, dust bowl, hit the road again blues
I got the dirt track, dust bowl, hit the road again blues.

Though you might not believe it from this poem, I really rather like Bangkok. It's a great place to sit around and do nothing. It is, of course, also rather sleazy.

Bangkok Hustle

They hassle you and hustle you
And strong-arm you and muscle you
And ply their art of getting to your cash.
They badger you and bother you
There's nothing they would rather do
Than get their grubby hands upon your stash.
The tuk-tuk drivers take you to
Anywhere they're wanting to
But never to the place you want to be.
Their uncle's cousin's brother has
Things they say no other has.
They take you to his shop and get their fee.

So, you do the Bangkok shuffle
As they Bangkok hustle
And you try to get away
Do you want to buy a T-shirt?
Want to buy a CD?
They hustle in your way.
You do the Bangkok shuffle
The side-step bustle
To get to where you want to go
Do you want to buy a necklace?
Want to see some boxing?
Want to see a ping-pong show?

And if you choose to walk along
You'll find the con-men going strong
With pitches cons and scams of every sort.
It's getting old to sell CDs
The current trick is MP3s
But bet there's nothing legal to be bought.
Or else men in suits and floral ties
Will smile and look you in the eyes
And offer gems at prices that can't fail,
Which you'll find, too late alas,
Are nothing more than coloured glass
By then your salesman's vanished on the trail.

So, you do the Bangkok shuffle
As they Bangkok hustle
And you try to get away
Do you want to buy a T-shirt?
Want to buy a CD?
They hustle in your way.
You do the Bangkok shuffle
The side-step bustle
To get to where you want to go
Do you want to buy a necklace?
Want to see some boxing?
Want to see a ping-pong show?

Markets are endlessly fascinating places. This is a description of the famous Kashgar Market in China.

Kashgar Market : These Things Define The Day

The air is filled with song and sound
from birds in bamboo cages.
Bent artisans shape wood and leather,
faces creased with age.
The lizard skins laid out and dried,
with powdered bone on wooden trays;
strange medicines and ancient cures:
these things define the day.

The strings of horses, sheep in pens
and cows and pigs and goats;
they whinny, bleat and grunt and call
a noise from every throat.
The hill folk dressed in blue and red,
the city men in grey,
the children, iridescent, bright:
these things define the day.

Cows' severed heads, the charnel stench,
the smoke from burning hides,
red rivulets that carve the dust
from road to riverside,
the withered old men gathered here,
the children at their play,
among the bloody carcasses:
these things define the day.

I've hiked the Inca Trail a couple of times and the first view of Machu Picchu from the Sun Gate is one of the world's great travel experiences. Getting there is something else though. It's really quite hard work.

<u>On The Inca Trail</u>
One step after another.
Raise a foot. Swing it forward.
Slam it down.
Breathe hard.
One step after another.
Back foot pulled from sucking mud
Clears the ground.
Breathe hard.
One step after another.
Stop.
Breathe hard.
Look up the hill at the miles to go.
Don't look back, no need to know
How little's gone.
Look at the rapidly receding back
Of the fastest fittest hiker on the track,
And then go on.
One step after another.
Try to keep a steady tread
Of laboured paces.
Breathe hard.
One step after another.
At every one you wish you were
In other places.
Breathe hard. One step after another.

Off the coast of Alaska we had a rather fruitless day whale watching – fruitless because for hours we saw lots of birds but nothing even vaguely similar to a whale. At last though, in the far distance one surfaced.

Haiku: Whale Watching in Alaska

Red winter eyes still scour
The cold horizon. Hours.
Finally a fluke.

There are some things that, while not pleasant, seem to be universal. Unfortunately one of those things is poverty.

The Invisible People of Prague

On the narrow cobbled streets
That thread between the
Baroquely beautiful towers
Of the city,
As smoothly as silk
Through a needle's eye,
They have become invisible.
Eyes fixed on elaborate cornices,
On the detail and the decoration,
On the elegant façades
Of a bygone century;
Eyes raised in praise
Of art and artifice,
Do not see them.
They kneel in the snow,
Silent and unmoving,
Foreheads pressed to the cold stone,
Empty caps upturned before them.
They are as still and grim
As the gargoyles that look down
In mocking mimicry.
They are as grey and snow covered
As the streets themselves.
And they are invisible.

And, the same is also true in England. Returning from Prague I walked around Birmingham where, in the subway, begging, was a teenaged girl.

Alice In The Underpass

Alice waking, Alice sleeping,
Alice laughing, Alice weeping,
Alice singing, Alice dancing,
Alice fleeing and advancing,
Alice trying, Alice failing,
Alice healthy, Alice ailing,
Alice wanting, Alice needing,
Alice broken, Alice bleeding,
Alice falling, Alice flying,
Alice living, Alice dying.
Alice through the looking glass.
Alice in the underpass.